Let's Visit Costa Rica

Weeee!!!

Publisher: Curious Kids Press, Palm Springs, CA 92264. All rights reserved.
Editor: Sterling Moss
Designed by: Michael Owens
Copy Editor: Janice Ross

Chapter 1: Hola! Welcome to My Awesome Country

My name is Hugo. I am 7 years old and I am in the second grade. Welcome to COSTA RICA!

I want to tell you about my country. I'll tell you about the geography, the people, and the many amazing animals – like this really cool frog. Can you guess what it's called? Scientists think the big red eyes help scare **predators** away.

Red-eyed Tree Frog

Words to Know

Predator (*noun*): An animal that lives by killing and eating other animals.

As you read this book, be sure to look for my pet toucan **"Tootie."**

Wherever you see **Tootie Toucan**, it means she has a **fun fact** about my country to tell you.

Tootie Toucan's Fun Fact

CROOOOAAK! Costa Rica means "rich coast" in Spanish.

Costa Rica is a small country in Central America.

The country is about the size of West Virginia in the United States.

COSTA RICA

West Virginia

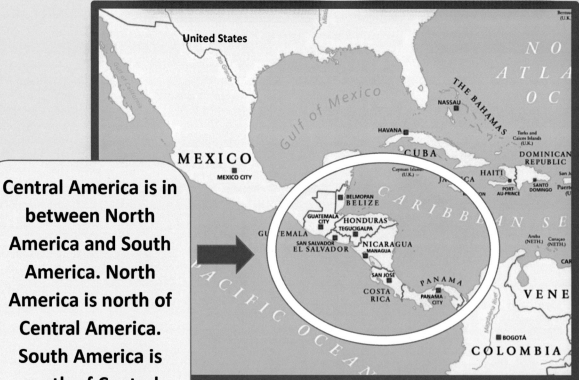

Central America is in between North America and South America. North America is north of Central America. South America is south of Central America.

There are seven countries in Central America. Look at the map. Can you name those seven countries? What two countries border Costa Rica?

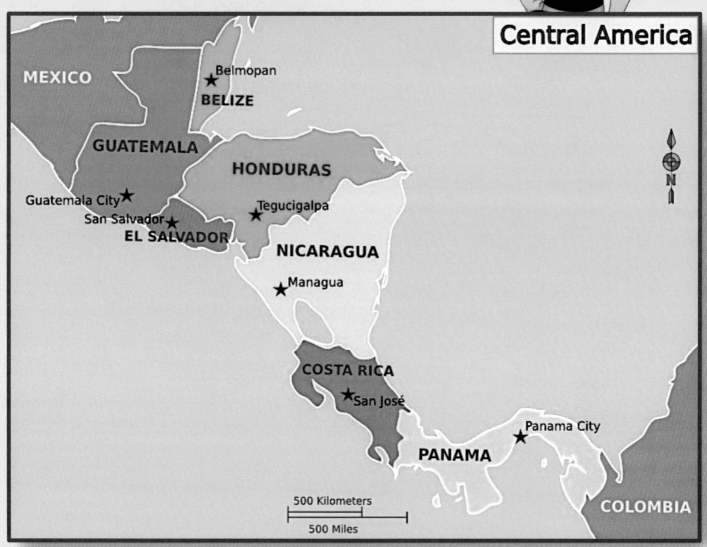

Words to Know

Border (*verb*): To be next to or lie on the boundary (or dividing line) of something.

Border (*noun*): The outside edge of something; boundary line.

The history of Costa Rica is really cool. It was "discovered" by Christopher Columbus.

Actually, there were other people living here before Columbus arrived. So, he didn't really *discover* it. But he was the first **European** to step foot in Costa Rica.

Land, Ahoy!

Words to Know

European (*noun*): A person from one of the countries in the continent of Europe.

Independent (*adjective*): Not ruled or controlled by another country.

Land, Ahoy!: A saying shouted from a ship at sea when land is spotted.

Four different tribes of people lived in Costa Rica when Columbus first arrived here. Over time, many died from diseases, such as smallpox or measles. They didn't have those diseases before the Europeans arrived.

Today, there are only a few **descendants** of those original people in Costa Rica.

Each year, at a special festival, descendants of the original people of Costa Rica perform a dance. It tells the story of how the Spanish conquered Costa Rica.

Words to Know

Descendant (*noun*): Someone related to a person or group of people who lived at an earlier time.

I live with my family in San Jose. San Jose is the capital of Costa Rica. It has about 300,000 people. That is the same size as Honolulu, Hawaii. How many people live in your city or town?

Costa Rica has many **tropical** rain forests. A rain forest has many tall trees. It is very warm and gets lots of rain. Many different kinds of plants and animals live in a rain forest.

Tootie Toucan's Fun Fact

The largest rain forest in the world is the Amazon rain forest in South America. Most of it lies in Brazil.

Words to Know

Tropical (*adjective*): Having to do with an area that has very warm temperatures throughout the year, usually 77 to 78 degrees Fahrenheit (25 to 28 degrees Celsius).

Costa Rica has amazing beaches. They are great for surfing, fishing, or playing in the sand or the ocean waves. The weather on the Pacific Coast is usually pretty hot and dry.

Tootie Toucan's Fun Fact

Costa Rica has two seasons. The dry season lasts from December to April. It hardly rains at all anywhere in Costa Rica during the dry season. The rainy lasts from May to December. It can rain almost every day. But, usually, the rain doesn't last very long.

Costa Rica also has many **volcanoes**. Some of these volcanoes are active. That means they could erupt at any time. People from all over the world come to visit the volcanoes.

Words to Know

Volcano (*noun*): A mountain that opens downward to a pool of melted rock below the surface of the earth. Sometimes pressure builds up. Eruptions occur. Gases and rock shoot up through the opening, They spill over the sides of the mountain or into the air.

Chapter 2: A Day in My Cool Life

Tonight, I got an e-mail from my friend Emma in America. She is also in the second grade. She wanted to know what my day was like. Here is what I told her.

5:30 a.m.

I got up early and got dressed for school.

Everyone at school wears a **uniform**. Boys wear blue pants or shorts and a white shirt. Girls wear blue pants or a blue skirt and a white shirt.

Words to Know

Uniform (*noun*): Specific clothing that is worn by all members of a group.

6:30 a.m.

My mother fixed my favorite breakfast. It's called *gallo pinto*. (Say: gah-yo PIN-toe). It's a mixture of white rice and black beans. It's served at almost every meal. I like to have it with eggs, cheese, and a tortilla.

Tootie Toucan's Fun Fact

Costa Ricans love tamales – especially at Christmas. Eating tamales at Christmas is like eating turkey at Thanksgiving in the United States.

7:00 a.m.

Then, I rode my bike to school. We have school every day, Monday through Friday. The school year begins in February. It finishes the last week in November. We are off in December and January. That's like your "summer vacation." We also get two weeks off in July.

2:00 p.m.

After school, I played fútbol with my friends. You call it soccer, but it's the same thing. Sofia and Luisa are the best players.

Then, I returned home and helped with chores around the house.

Tootie Toucan's Fun Fact

In Costa Rica, everyone loves soccer. Even the smallest towns have a soccer field. What's your favorite sport?

7:00 p.m.

For dinner we had **casado**. That's rice and beans and meat or chicken or fish. After supper, I did my homework. Estoy estudiando inglés.

18

9:00 p.m.

So, that was my day. Tomorrow, is Saturday. We are going to Manuel Antonio National Park for the weekend. It will be lots of fun. I'm sure I will fall asleep dreaming about ziplining at the park tomorrow.

Tootie Toucan's Fun Fact
Ziplines are made up of steel cables. The cables are strung above the rain forest between two platforms. You can zoom across the **canopy** on a zipline from one platform to another. It's lots of fun!

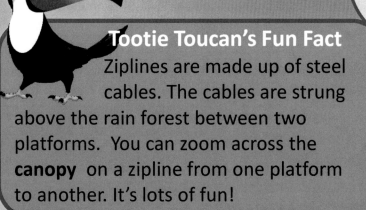

Words to Know

Canopy (*noun*): The upper part of the trees in a rain forest. Monkeys, sloths, and many different birds live in the canopy.

Chapter 3: The Amazing Wildlife of Costa Rica

One of the really cool things about my country is all of its animals. Here is what our teacher told us.

In Costa Rica, there are more than 200 **reptiles**.

There are hundreds of mammals.

There are nearly 1,000 different birds.

Words to Know

Mammal (*noun*): Animals that produce live young rather than laying eggs.

Reptile (*noun*): A group of animals like snakes, turtles, lizards, and crocodiles that have very short legs or none at all.

One of my favorite animals is the sloth. They can be found hanging upside down in the tropical rain forests of Costa Rica

Tootie Toucan's Fun Fact

Sloths spend almost their entire lives hanging upside down in a tree. They eat, sleep, and even give birth upside down.

We have four different **species** of monkeys in Costa Rica. The `Capuchin Monkey` is one. Capuchin monkeys are very smart. They use "tools," such as stones, to crack open shell fish.

The Capuchin Monkey is also known by another name. Can you guess what it is? Look at its face for a clue.

Words to Know
Species (*noun*): Kind; a group of similar living things.

The **Mantled Howler Monkey** is another one of the four different monkeys in Costa Rica. It is famous for its howl. It can be heard 1 mile (1.6 km) away.

Tootie Toucan's Fun Fact

There are more Howler Monkeys in Costa Rica than any other.

Another monkey in Costa Rica is the **Spider Monkey.** It is the largest monkey in Costa Rica. Look at its long tail. It uses its long tail like another hand or leg. Pretty cool, huh?

Tootie Toucan's Fun Fact
The tail of a Spider monkey is longer than its head and body.

The **Squirrel Monkey** is the smallest monkey in Costa Rica. Some say it got its name because it looks like a squirrel. What do you think?

Tootie Toucan's Fun Fact

The word monkey in Spanish is "mono."

More Books Just for You from
Curious Kids Press

Check out these fun-to-read books about countries and cultures around the world, as well as other high-interest nonfiction books from Curious Kids Press.

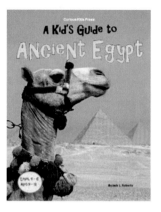

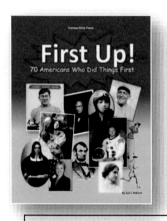
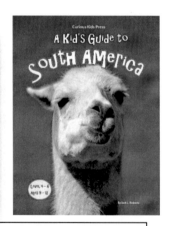

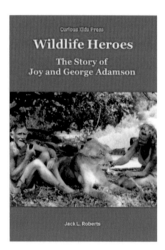

Ages 9 - 12; Levels 4 - 6

For more information, visit: www.curiouskidspress.com

Let's Visit
Costa Rica
For Parents and Teachers

About This Book

Let's Visit . . . is an engaging, easy-to-read book series that provides an exciting adventure into fascinating countries and cultures around the world for young readers. Each book focuses on one country, continent, or U.S. territory, and includes colorful photographs, informational charts and graphs, and quirky and bizarre "Did You Know" facts, all designed to bring the country and its people to life. Designed primarily for recreational, high-interest reading, the informational text series is also a great resource for students to use to research geography topics or writing assignments.

About the Reading Level

Let's Visit. . . is an informational text series designed for kids in grades K-3, ages 5 to 8. For some young readers, the series will provide new reading challenges based on the vocabulary and sentence structure. For other readers, the series will review and reinforce reading skills already achieved. While for still other readers, the book will match their current skill level, regardless of age or grade level.

About the Author

 **Jack L. Roberts** began his career in educational publishing at Children's Television Workshop (now Sesame Workshop), where he was Senior Editor of The Sesame Street/Electric Company Reading Kits. Later, at Scholastic Inc., he was the founding editor of a high-interest/low-reading level magazine for middle school students. Roberts is the author of more than a dozen biographies and other non-fiction titles for young readers, published by Scholastic Inc., the Lerner Publishing Group, Teacher Created Materials, Benchmark Education, and others.. More recently, he was the co-founder of WordTeasers, an educational series of card decks designed to help kids of all ages improve their vocabulary through "conversation, not memorization."

Made in the USA
Lexington, KY
04 April 2018